LOST HORIZON

Lost Horizon © Nathaniel Farrell, 2019

ISBN 978-1-946433-25-1
First Edition, First Printing, 2019

Ugly Duckling Presse
The Old American Can Factory
232 Third Street #E-303
Brooklyn, NY 11215
www.uglyducklingpresse.org

Distributed by SPD / Small Press Distribution

Cover image: Basement floorplan (detail), Westroads Mall (current site of
St. Louis Galleria), Karasek Architects Collection. Courtesy of the Missouri
Historical Society, St. Louis, Missouri. (Image color altered from original.)

Cover design by Kyra Simone and Don't Look Now!
Typeset in Dante and Frutiger by Doormouse

Books printed offset and bound in the USA by McNaughton & Gunn

The publication of this book was made possible, in part, by a grant from
the National Endowment for the Arts, and by the continued support of
the New York State Council on the Arts.

Nathaniel Farrell

LOST HORIZON

Ugly Duckling Presse, 2019

The fountain full of coins   the smell of pretzels, print, perfume

formaldehyde in fabrics

                brass rails down stairwells   rebar in the pillars

the underground parking structure — Roman alphabet
                                        Arabic numerals —

red carpet in the cineplex lobby
subterranean systems of concrete cisterns and piping

a drop of water   a flake of light: all that remains of home

                        in the mountain
                        beneath the mountain

                        the seas beneath the seas others name

pushed and pulled by the moon   its dark tunnel into outer space where

gravity pulls light
                        around a vanishing point

small as a pin prick and as lost as
                        a grain of sweat in the lines of a human hand.

Boyfriends   girlfriends
                    gone to the toilets down the corridor

path of the finger trowel through the mortar

                              between cinder blocks: pecked

gritstone
or stony kernels from the gristmill stone.

                              Beneath the brick

the beach stretches around bubbles in the sand.

                         A sand-bug wiggles like a fingerprint.

Pyramid, profile, three-quarter profile — the different shades to

                         nickels and necks. Sex of a penny-flip:

tailor's dummy   seamstress's shape   choice of birthday motifs,
                                                centerpiece.

          The little prince's balloon wanders with his wrist

the ribbon's knot is small and tight. I say I will call when I'm ready.

At the tea party: polite questions about
                              new stitches in an old animal.

Through the flatware section, through support pillars plated with mirror

display cases backlit — sweet air:

              gardenia   peony   rose
              sandalwood   ambergris, civet musk
              that contrasting rancid note.

The intercom opens. I eavesdrop.
                              I gesture "No thank you."

Little dimples of light distort in the glass:

              a vial, a bottle, a message, a wish
a pendant
                                        a little stick fish.

Tennis balls on walker legs — condensation in the skylights

last year's drop ceiling in the ivy

              tufted chintz seats
              near three-ways between fitting rooms

rub of cloth against upholstery. Fragrance models

the tall stools at the cosmetics counter

spritzers anticipant
at dueling stations

mons veneris   mademoiselle   décolletage   scent strips

a dab of Chanel or Shalimar —

or the male model's hairless thighs
the poignant angle of his bulge.

The skin on the meat of my thumb ripples under the hand dryer

ripples over the bones on the back of my hand.
(Code Adam over the store speakers.)

Sale at the anchor space
study of retail landscape:

Toys "R" Us off the exit ramp

a family in Sunday dress clothes —

wires and straps
hold the growing saplings straight.

Lilyturf ground cover   Spanish moss soil topper

bails of hay stacked in the store window
holograms on hat brims

a garland of starfish   oscillating fan

inspection stickers
a foal's wet nose in a handful of oats — bristle of whiskers.

More quarters for the traffic meter, the Tower Optical viewer,
more pellets at the petting zoo

another turn on the carousel.

The tertiary colors
of toy shovels

faded plastic playsets   summer after summer

peeling in the backyard like skin from a sunburn —

corona in the sprinkler's spray
a thumb over the garden hose

The home gardener presses
spikes of Miracle-Gro into the mulch bed. Casual Fridays.

It takes many tries to make it through
                    the same kind of day over and over,

to learn the names of people or Power Rangers. One of the tiny screws

            slowly undoes itself from one of the temples on my glasses.

The Elf King's daughter
                    through the porte-cochère

        couches in the garden house

                    the babysitter's squirrelly little shorts
                    ashiver in the A/C — pet names under threat

through the mist past Victoria's Secret. Bombshell:

floral   fruity
notes of purple passion fruit, Shangri-La peony, vanilla, orchid,

and jasmine. Ring marks on the nightstand   on the ring finger

                    lace doily   polyester or nylon mesh

nymphet   fishnet   finishing touch   tampon flushed.

(Some say "parking meter." Some say "multiplex" or "Kleenex.")

Foot Locker boys at magnetic checkpoints

party dresses in plastics   star-studded jeans
embroidered or stenciled   click-click of untied shoelaces

brass separators between terrazzo squares   waxed and polished

     plant leaves dusted —

how the cloth leaves momentary streaks, how the streaks are

     vanishing. Lingerie sales assistant

     tailor's tape over her shoulder

bust   hips   waist   arm length   chest   shoulders   inseam

     "Are they like apples, oranges,
cantaloupes, or watermelons?"

Binary programs anticipate the changes in temperature:

     revolving door ordinance   rubber whoosh,

Escalator teeth fit into each other neatly

     smell of graphite lubricant.

A cellphone glows in a back pocket —

          paisley ties spread in rays on the display island

beach outfits; ultrasound

                    foamy like peroxide or

the Gulf Stream spinning on the flat-screen. Laugh tracks

             nature documentaries   meteorologists
                    making their motions

metamorphosis of water, land, spines, furrows. With or without

leaf over sex   topographic map   vines in locks of pool-wet hair —

          promise ring   acne medication   satellite footage

plastic bags   post-consumer cardboard carryout boxes

                tentacles. In the large eyes of the virgins
                  what they'd call "dewy loins."

Small eyes of the monster the color of steamed vegetables.

      There are fossils of ocean life in
            the Great Plains. There's

a difference between   fishermen and anglers, between

a small town
and a small-town experience.

A cellphone glows in a back pocket   in another back pocket

x's and o's flung from the inland orchard
drift back to earth like slug's trails

glisten through rows of strawberry.

Fan fiction — full stop. Born-agains in the back seat of the retreat bus:

genitalia twists in their guts like love letters

rent then snatched by the wind-tossed tongue that tickles the dog-
eared corners of the pages

or crumpled like the pile of snow
in the empty parking spaces

around an island near the main exit

light poles sticking up
like masts on a sinking ship —

more snow presses grass flat along the riverbanks.

The water flows backwards with the tide

holds memory still for a moment then shakes the branch to its fork

up through the creek system

to more melting snow   gloomy

brilliant over pinched rocks. In the drugstore parking lot

red vending machines for movies

sliding doors   superhero noblesse   more soft rubber
soft slam of the car door.

Barn swallows roost under the gas station canopy.

Soft earth at the spring's source:

limestone   sandstone   velvet rope   skipping stone

a pebble's plunk

among hearts
heavy as boulders in a stony stream.

River mud tugs
at the hunter's boot.

Vultures tug tendons from the bone.

Copyrights   credits   placards. Exhibition labels
in the American Landscape room   the seismograph in the corner —
                    its tiny needle trembles.

I leave a message anyway.

Patches of roadkill   rumble strips   gift shops

crusted scaffolding stacked in the back of a flatbed

                            advanced tickets.

The apples are wet; the branch bends when it's pulled —

                    The air under the tree
                    fermenting fruit and soil and

Eve's heart heavy as a sofa-bed. Old well-damp air:

parachute pods drift in the dapples   maple-tree helicopters
float down into the dark hump of earth

            its brocade of hard-hearted pearls along seams

beads and sequins on the sleeves of an evening dress.

Water   a ribbon
          between red bricks, fieldstone:

watermarks on stationery

          reach down to the silver dollar.

Chokecherries collect in birdbaths   stain the stone — lichen in

     the nooks and crannies of lawn statues.

          Pygmalion — Pocahontas

no oiled braids, no smell of suede

          pink or blue pagoda in fine oriental toile

the bark of shadows   to-be buds

     whisper
     of the chisel at the breast of unblushing marble
          polished bronze.

Through stained-glass windows   lead ribs   parasol ribs the curves of other curves

brainy intestines

dress sizes, ring sizes, waist lines —

Kay's or Jared's

felt fingers point like
little cream-colored penises

anemones planted in coral bark as living rock.

The smell of saliva on a pillow.

Some people have bad stars
and so spiral out of themselves

path of an arm within an arm —

cases of multiple identities

souls shaken until one falls out, unfolds like an ink blot

or else they come apart
like the cording around the edge of a mattress.

Drive-thru tellers   the decline of pneumatic tubes.

Hubble points other-worldward

a dimmer switch for the chandelier.

Leaf cut in the urinal

through the urine-soaked paper of

a half-peeled cigarette butt rolling around

the plastic cage for the mint in the saga of clean water

starry fruit   humidity   heat index

the torch on the back of dimes

Eternal Flame of Arlington

tar-thick lungs of coastal bedrock —

a dry cleaner's tag still pinned to my inner pocket.

Wind moves the leaves; leaves
move the branches back and forth

in the reflecting pool in the lobby, the clearing:

ficus, brasswork, smooth gray stones in a glass vase
selected for their smoothness.

Naturally green clay tennis court or

                                           painted asphalt.

      Skin stretched tight over the shinbone.

                    Optic yellow felt, white latticework   AstroTurf

down the steps   the touch of an unfinished TIG weld in

                               the crook of the hand rail

imprint of a necklace on the bosom or a hem   a tan line —

                little hairs pinched in a watch clasp.

Bellboy   luggage cart   casino-grade carpet   curlicues the color

                          of Veuve Clicquot.

Ski gear. Wind shear. Trolleys and lifts   scenic pull-offs

                in the valley   the Wal-Mart

                             a barracks for

RVs parked out near the dumpsters near the exit

                  plastic recycling numbers

    . corresponding polymers. Fluorescent tubes pop in the dumpster.

A cashier spins the bagging spindle, licks her finger

                                        spreads the edges
                                        divides the handles.

Cardboard car fresheners twist in the wind
            through car windows a crack open —

                        steering wheels
                        sticky from the sun

                        post-mount spotlights

                        gimbals   gyroscope navigation system —

Mercury in retrograde   so inclined, Mercury

                                        a smudged fingerprint

            on the ball-top joystick

one-player, two-player buttons   splash screen   top score initials

playoff brackets in marker or chalk. A plushie slips free of the claw.

            Lightbulb aisle. Color-matching swatches.

Garden hose pin stripe —

pearl-gray, Magid brand, leather-palm work gloves with safety cuff welder's glass   router bits

paper cutters at the Fed-Ex office, laminated menus,

arrows pulse down the stipe reader

call for showers over the intercom —

water pressure   PSI range   compression rate
                coin-operated weight scale

yesterday's and today's winning lottery numbers.

Railroad tie lawn ideas   tractor tire herb gardens

ceramic or terracotta

trucker's arm   water-resistant devices   quick-dry bathing suits.

Train buffs wait near the crossing.

Holsteins   Limousins.

Rubber switch, flop over, run-through, hand-thrown, spring.

Two-story ice cream cones. At the state park

boat launch, the lake sloshes up around the trailer tires

over the hash lines. At night

sometimes

skinny-dippers' clothes hang from the branches

shoes stuffed with socks

time pieces   cologne on the collars.

The clouds at night are shaved thin and curly —
greeny tips of morning glory

reach up the road sign   out from the maple branches
hanging over the creek's dark eddies.

Single-lane bridge, castle-shaped restaurant —

bobbing buttocks   hair wet halfway up a strange girl's back

twinkle of wet toes
beads on the eyelashes and elbows   the trapezius muscle

clavicles under shore-ruffled moonlight, moonlight ruffled spring:

mustard seed field
soybean field
cow pasture

historic downtown —

brushstroke; breaststroke. Water low in the reservoir around
the Shavertown steeple.

(Some say "soft as cornsilk.")

Patches of blood-caked fur. A squirrel   guts squeezed out its mouth.

My stomach twists in the crochet needle.

The rules of the Pepacton watershed. Rivets in the bottom of
the rowboat — sinkholes in lawn

a whirlpool in the lake down the drill-line
into the Great Lake salt mine

before the area code changed. Before LEDs or stockpeople —

personal checks   cash-only establishments   classic hut
architecture

jukebox design. Rain carries grass seed down the hill
and under the door in the mud. From the mud

a tuft of grass,
from the bulb, a tuber.

The Delawares of Oklahoma.

Lovers' names carved in the ferryboat deck rail —

love locks on the bridgework   keys tossed into the river

sparkle at first from the bottom.

White blaze of Xenon or halogen.

Droplets of water on the windshield
twitch like pond skaters.

Penny wishes corrode on the tile
smelling of chlorine and copper.

The fountain drained

the river spreads through the delta, a hydra —

the moon bears down, cleaves the river in channel after channel
guides each into the ocean.

The estuary pushes the river back with the tide. Tabloid print

tin-can telephones   prize-winning melons.

The earth's track is wide.

Once there was a people who said that
the sun was drawn by horse team

horizon to horizon
stabled in oat-colored twilight   the colors of
Canadian money

or the new Jacksons
Ben Franklin's holographic bell in the inkwell.

Acorns, sweetgum pods. A family runs toward their car

holding umbrellas against the windy rain
their trousers darken around their thighs.

Proper posture of men in the portrait signing
the Declaration of Independence

or the recklessness of the Last Supper.

Gothic Renaissance. In the nave   the formal name

a portrait of life moving or the portrait of a moving life:

hair grows down backs, around faces, down arms and legs —
plants grow toward the sun.

Votaries   pet birds   pre-game coverage

aerosol field stripes   game regulations
                    goal post pads with Velcro fasteners.

Asphalt ripples in the hot hue of cheerleader vertigo:
                              sunspot-dotted eyes

bleachers   human pyramids   outdoor bathrooms.

        The top of the vet's hat sunk to his scalp
                          heavy with pins and buttons —

bags of ice slapped on concrete
                    dumped in a cooler.

            Federal holiday first Monday   last Monday.

Bug spray, sunscreen, Calamine lotion.

                The mud is silky; the water
                clear until someone wades in

        scatters tadpoles warming in the shallows.

Brown and yellow signs   yellow and white signs   RV hookups.

Someone gets a splinter from the picnic bench. Someone
strikes a match
        heats a needle in the flame — the tip
                glows briefly in the flame.

I wait at the bathrooms;

          they smell of the feces and orange cleanser

              Yankee Candle.

Someone's son or daughter swims to the dock. Minnows
                come to test their toes

heads like shards of green ice or broken auto glass.

         Bigger fishes cruise in the sun and scum.

My headache grows leaner.

Carp pile on top of each other at the Pymatuning spillway; carp
    grab at pieces of crust
        torn up and tossed

              overhand   underhand.

Ducks near the outer edge of the frenzy.

The grass is strange on the bank —

bags of stale bread for sale at the visitor center

coin-operated binoculars tick, wind back

boat rentals   pavilion reservations

flush toilets   showers   emergency call stations
calendar of dangers, safety tips

horsepower regulations
proper storage and disposal of foodstuffs   refuse. Printout photos

illustrate regional wildlife and weather
colored paper   colored fonts

time out   pick-up spots

antiquing brochures
auto sales circulars
farm-fresh markets.

Slow moving vehicle signs on the Amish buggies.

IHOP   Denny's   a sign for Hooter's at the Colonial Williamsburg exit

the owl's eyes made to look like nipples —

period dress waitresses:

        jogging shorts   halter tops

          or a Bavarian barmaid's bodice and apron

business cards
swimsuit calendars   kickball umpires   reenactments.

        Lifeguards cute as
           the dimples in the park ranger's hat.

Stench of snakes

          fingers dirty from a snack.

The heavy weight of the lake and me
       rooted as a grub buried in the lake bottom.

Susquehanna   Chesapeake   Patuxent   Potomac   Rappahannok

        Piankatank
        York
        James

Yellow foam floats in the harbor. Flotsam finds the corners
of the marina. Gulls on the cable dishes, radio masts —

squall line like a wall against the tall ships show.

Or at the Tiki bar, the Polynesia Islander Revue
                    sarongs and leis.

Manila twine to hang the business hours; wooden signs

                    outside the cafe, outside the keepsake shop

cursive letters written in rope
                              studded with scallop shells.

          Pewter figurines marshalled to the high ground.

Boarding announcement for ships in a bottle
                              Middle Passage frigate model

     strings pulled from the mouth of the jug.

               Prohibition schooners.

                    Rain blooms moss. The frosty polish
on a bottle once tossed true into a true current —

moss soft as the hair on the skin between knuckles. Fables of
children found after being lost.

County wetlands drained by developers

permits posted. The foreman's trailer on blocks —

clerks talk about the outlets. The wait staff in black slacks sings
"Happy Birthday"
or "Feliz Cumpleaños."

Between bumper block and asphalt

bolts eroded by the Ice Melt — a field of railroad ties stacked in bails.

In the river's silt
the mountain's pride: a twist in a rope

a bolt of overgrowth. Only the longest or shortest waves pass through us

radio waves   gamma-rays. Puddles near the curb as the

milky arms of our galaxy spread wider
while windmill farms
scatter bird shit like fine flour.

Avocado.   TV as diorama or diocese   catfish farms   trout hatchery.

Green and purple mountains
wear down the painter's brush.

Beach breakers   destroyer ships   bobby socks   Mason lodges

grasshoppers   foot-high pies   heat lamps   grasp of apron strings.

                    Cigarette burns on the waitress' arm

cash tip. Coal-tar compounds

                    break down
                    settle or evaporate.

I never dream that any specific person can hurt me.

          White marks in the fingernails move toward the tip:

                    little lies that also pass with time.

Peninsulas   Florida and Michigan

                              residential subdivisions in bulbs
around the bypasses — the geographical range of seabirds or

                    lemmings in a sleepless burrow

dismally dwindling
          through literal and metaphorical winters.

          Orange safety fencing near the tee-off to the putting green.

The swampy tongue of the bog turns the corpse like a lozenge:

wood   bone   leather   flint.

An eel writhes through tall grass
          writes in dry land on its way to the Sargasso Sea
             far from where it used to be.

          Volcanos leave island craters as the earth passes over
          the mantle's plume.

Frost burns shrubs into crystals. Hairy roots:

the rise and fall of witchcraft

             spells to speak to the dead or
          to prevent the dead from speaking.

Stiff fingers pry apart peat, wiggle through the culvert
          out toward the housing development.

A golf ball cut by the mower blade.

          Bog people dug up in Denmark or Windover
          return through a door in the dig site.

Greenhouses — tax forms
          migration patterns of the early settlers   causes of death

the rise and fall of gameshow hosts

                                        their beautiful
                                        assistants.

                        In the breakroom
                        the skill of unfolding
                        and refolding newspapers.

Between rhizomes and roots,

                                between polishing and sharpening.

Concrete hangs on the plywood form   sawdust in
                                the gullet between face-ground teeth.

                A bit of fur caught in barbed wire. Over the land bridge
the herds once grazing rootless
                                        distance fed.

Wintered fences creak —
                        tractor tracks
                                crease the field.

Enemy armor sinks on the bog
                like the plastic pieces of board games or wizard wands.

Bubbles creep up through the soil   through a threshold
                             of string and stakes.

              Tea roses bloom in the alley.

Bees gather pollen in the botanical garden
          foxfire flares orange and
                        green. Red beacons

blink on the hill. From the root of the city

a siren grows louder, grows faint as others take its place
                       until blue sky
              covers the stars.

I read about
      those greener paradises of hope, those pleasant slopes
                   somewhere in the Himalayas

        somewhere back through the treacherous pass

the stinging wind   storm's warmth known by the guide

like a beekeeper knows the quality of the swarm   the hive

seen from far off
as though the Earth from a satellite or
              through the walls of the killing jar:

a circle and a tree   a leaf

rhododendron-colored smear of nebula   the face of the astronaut

pressed against the porthole glass   a headpiece in the portico stone —

alien visitations

                    smell of canine in the cushions

a trio of dancing dolphins   Busby Berkeley numbers   high divers
taking the shortest distance between two points.

                   Colors squirm on the backs of my eyelids,
            dash over the television screen —

through the hum   the approach of a fingertip   the bite of that
little blue worm wiggling out of ash and crackling wind.

                 Knock on the screen and it would sound

thick as the shape of dinosaur names twisting in folds of brain

               blank as a far-off continent, a far away

smudge of lipstick on a tissue or
              the breathy, humid smell of tears —

a twig for the monarch caterpillar or wooly bear
to hang its chrysalis on. Everything far away:

planks of the boardwalk seeded with pretzel salt

cigarette ash
yellowjackets at the trash cans

sticky melt of popsicles   burn marks
gum spots   spit stains

ants all over the lollipop — stiff new
hot-press T-shirts

clack of poster racks   roller doors.

A wedding party mills around

waiting on the magic hour.

Children on the beach dig a hole to China

take a drink of lemonade; dig a hole to China
take a drink of lemonade.

Lifeguard whistles   one-pieces — piles of seaweed

unfinished coloring books   truck testicles
        tangled yarn   cartoon-faced backpacks.

        How silent the last gaspless breath

of the mermaid's watery death — and she so scolded
        for loving someone with mud in his heart.

The sound of a clamshell
        popped open in the video store aisle.

        Sky-shaped ceiling fans.

Spermy smell of the Bradford pear —

stamen   spray   petals splayed on windshield wipers:

outer space dangles its spores. Iridescent

        land masses   weather patterns

sea level   Tyvek stapled to the frame   the magnolia unwhorled —

        oak-tree catkins

ants over earthworms half-dead on the sidewalk
        until nothing's left but a brittle brown curl.

Radio antennas pump on the horizon

       signal some new story in the Channellocks.

I walk the dog to the gazebo and back.

           Delicate hair color   spring break

   online dating portfolios   family-friendly surfing

Emergency Alert Systems   safe harbor hours.

         The wax is hottest around the wick.

The building I live in
       has brick
          the color of skin on a popped blister.

Leftovers crust up on the countertops — a dried spill
           on a placemat of the world

seaside wandering up and down its coasts

        traced with a fork tine

or the bumping of the brigantine against landfall. A phone number
   in ballpoint on a soft piece of forearm.

Or these lashes   weapons swung
                against the unkissed regions of selhood.

     Barge lowered   horses tethered.

                   Mountains turn to silt among
the shells   the ocean's little toes wiggle in the surf.

       A grounds crew tends the unplanted hill.

Birds perch on headstones like any other stones. Marble
gets softer with weather —

               veins of quartz bulge out around
               letters growing shallow.

Blue-ruled clouds crumpled
          in red lines left by folds in the pillowcase.

Dead vines wound up through the chain-link.

Twist-off bottle caps,   pieces of crushed lighters
                  turnpike franchises.

A century of sky through aqueducts   castles   tour guides —

the warp of the course's pitch and yaw   central celestial point
above the sand trap

reflection of one planet on another

triangulation of targets   first-stage reforestation

in the empty speedway   paving cracked by weed colonies

saplings sprung through grass as
        Queen Anne's Lace grows up its curved bank.

National Weather Service
        time and temperature: the voice of Paul or Donna.

        A swarm of midges spirals in the air at dusk

chirps whittle dawn from dark branches.

          Blankets of morning glories
          thrown over the fences re-open in the gloom.

Trimmings of fingernails: the dry curl of shaved wood. Calcified

        in soft tissue   oxidized copper elbows or

                that horses snarl in statues

bronze plaque: employee handbook

                    author contract   needle exchange. Inky roots

through the fungal network, through
          the tickling wind of the world wide web. Cable lines
                              strung down the state route

twirled cursive around
telephone poles   mailboxes on 4x4 posts   tiger lilies
                                        in the roadside ditch.

Snapping turtle

              well-house   corrugated roof   tarred footer —

the ghosts of insects and summer
                              grow delicate and slender.

          That monarchs fly south to Mexico

that copper horses snarl greenly   gold spear tips on the flags
mounted residence to residence.

              Creosote fenceposts   more distance

terminal towers   commuter lane   roadside noise barriers

wild violet in the knotweed

             laundry hung on a line strung

across the lawn:
      the weight of jeans, the weight of jeans and water

           a roll of quarters

personalized return labels.

        The hotel staff speaks through the door —
omni-directional surveillance cameras
           in the elevator and hallways

helmet cams, body cams —

             accounting for wind speed

    leaves moving   dust raised
        branches swaying   water whitecapping.

Chipseal shimmers in the heatwave.

        Drop-wires sway in
          the courtyard.

The woof of dogs near the wharf   three-phase transmission lines

        between substations   ribbed bushing

old glass capacitors turn up near the creek
                                    ruddy from runoff

out from the strip mine

                        through the stumps of storm-cracked trees.

B&B cabins and lodges   cottages and bungalows   beachside
                        ocean currents pull person from person —

pierced voice   a stray paperclip from the bottom of the drawer

flecks of starlight and quartz: melatonin   photosynthesis.

                        Stinging mist sews together sheets of rain

                  plague   sinew   belly-rings
                  food court midriffs   wallet chains.

Gods and goddesses once sometimes went disguised as strangers.

                  At the Disney kiosk, the faces of princesses on
                  blankets folded blue and pink.

Smell of dust on lightbulbs   tissue paper.

            Patter of

a powder dauber in the rouge like Morse code —
the uncanny posture of children

their knack for espionage, for
speaking to animals, giants, dragons.

Small vinyl flags mark the utility lines
stems rusting in the irrigation route. Sewer systems

building codes   triceps. The walls of the storm drain curved
around the shape of a man.

Continental shelf follows highway
strip mall follows highway —

wind against hazard lights.

Free-speech blog fodder. Murk-water
the swampy squares of highway royalties.

Drum roll on a card-table in the grass. Condiment bottle
paperweights.

Relatives   co-workers
scraping teeth over corncobs

dessert
jiggles on the serving spatula —

the tack of fresh ice   Dixie cups

      how children like to crush them in their small hands.

Bottle rockets. Sprites and cherubs posed in statue —

      the life and times of well-known garden gnomes:

          Martin with a lantern   Erich the Gardner
        Balduin the mushroom farmer   Instus with wheelbarrow

Willi with his favorite book. Marcus Aurelius   equestrian or

          Diana with her bow   breasts exposed:

she points her arrow to the sky. There are
      hunting hounds lean around her legs.

          A wing juts from the fuselage into
        a khaki   white horizon.

Open-back blouses, open-neck collars   horsefly stylets

     ants through concrete   termites through wood

ivy over the retaining wall. Broken snaps on baseball caps —

complimentary WiFi in the cabin

Southern Heritage battle-flag bikini.

Sasquatch lurches through the yard ornament catalog.

Nothing matters in every parallel timeline.

From
a lump of coal from the mine stuck in the creek-bed mud:

the chthonic rituals of Canaanites.

Duck decoys among mystical creatures.

Daniel Boone waits at the salt lick.

Earth-dwellers. Latin or Greek conjugation of the verb "to rape"

in the brittle documents of history — their rectangular folds
and foxing.

Squeak of a drink straw. Paper-shredders bind up on staples.

A rubber band shaped like a footprint in wet concrete.
More expensive gravel near the entrance.

Greeting cards remote in time

like the sound of prop planes through little wildernesses

grid-locked orbits or
      our initials on a tree-stump.

        Pearl's sheen   turtle's carapace

mussel shell's blotted swirl   conch's inward pull —

          the rudder crushed by a careless tail fluke

hope cut to kindling in the starry ocean.

Cargohold   Asteroid   Centipede   Battle Axe   Beast Master

      a bit of light bounces out of the pupil like a laser.

Red eyes in the photo the color of frozen salmon —

        cellophane   three-ring binders.

County seat — bail bondsmen   title loans   pawn shop
      typewriter repair shop   recruiting office.

      Down the block from the courthouse

the saloon doors creak   the beaded curtain swings. A hula dancer
      parts the grass skirt with her hip —

the bomb grins like a shark down into the island's heart.

                                 Gold tassels on flagpoles caught by the wind.

Mermaid hair blowing in the tides at sunset

                curled in pensive currents in and around a bouldered shore.

        American bald eagle
wings addorsed and inverted, the U.S. flag in its talons.

Cheshire cat   dancing bear   a swallow diving under the North Star
                                   or with the moon in its beak

     skull and crossbones.

        And Alice's foot no bigger than a candle flame —

a white and blue frond. Someone pokes their straw around in melting ice.

     Songbirds   sailor girl with
                       dagger or banner.

     arm behind her head   arms akimbo   half akimbo
fluffing hair

          on tiptoe or odalisque.

Annie Oakley as anime hero
   Wonder Woman with her Lasso of Truth.

With one eye Alice looks through the door to the garden —

       Marsyas' flesh pinned back
to the bark of the tree. Lion, rampant, candy-apple red

        gorilla, sejant.

Aztec eagle warrior Amazon warrior Mayan face with tongue
   Celtic cross St. George's Cross

Zapata with bandoliers saltire. Realist portrait of Malcolm X
    or an arm sable couped bendwise.

Two wings, conjoined in lure — Jesus of Nazareth

   Pantocrator crucified sacred heart
       Man of Sorrows.

Polka-dot headscarf fruit hat feathered warbonnet

     underboob mandala, chandelier, lotus flower.

The faces of lost sons, daughters, lovers, never-agains

                              haunting the skin of the living.

Captain America   Jessica Rabbit   Planned Parenthood.

Snakes   vines   anchor and rope   anchor and wheel
anchor and compass — a thorny rose

peacock's eye   hen's eye in the snake's skull socket.

                                        Tinctures   pigments   furs

Holy feathers   dissolved in blackest filigree.

                              Storyboard: a dreamcatcher
                              turns in the window breeze

from over the field's loam   once cool and damp with corn
                              between the what's-it tree
                                        and the thistle's plume.

Streetlamps dot dark car doors. Bags of mulch stacked up
                              a backyard over against the tawny fence —

some neighbors live under others. Grasshoppers seem to fly.

A hiker inhabits the trail. Rock inhabits the body   the planet.

                    Through the tent's mesh window

the sounds of stalking curiosity.

Duck Hunter   Deer Hunter   licensed pinball tables

     video strip poker   Jägermeister   turquoise and silver curios —

Man in the Moon pajama print. A dollar bill folded in fours   mosquitos.

     Head and shoulders of an American Indian proper
     crowned with a plume of feathers.

Border patrol   toll-booths   checkpoints   inspection mirrors.

     Rotting grain in the corners of the empty silo

dry mud from the tire tread.

     Fortune-cookie fortunes
     under a magnet on the fridge.

Once-great beasts grope the barrens. Once-great chevrons bent

     the city's tint   its tangled sounds —

air conditioners groan, drip on awnings or sidewalks.

     Car horns

chatter of updraft ventilators — the stir-fry spins

with basil and lemongrass, choice of protein. Milk crates
bent from break time.

Sodium lights hum against the fire escape
window grate. Bolt turned bar set

door chain leaf-blowers scatter of flocks of crows

hospital zone school zone

pilot lights in the furnace

pink pistachio fingers

rubber bands rolled down a folded newspaper.

An empty box of teabags. Others
in their own insomnias other insects around other lights

other drops caught
in other screen doors other wood wet under the porch

The dog circles the spot it sits in —

the fact that a human touch
is not only a touch among humans.

Pieces of acorn tracked indoors
                    the straw in the new broom is a greener hue.

Paint rubs off the action figures lost a yard over; paint flecks
                                        off bricks.

Snow through the screens
                    spackles porch furniture.

            How amazing the damage a pure heart can do.

Tools rust in the shed
        in the cold ivory arms of winter ivy
                    childless

witches and evil mothers
        unwelcome suitors   psychiatrist appointments.

                        Winter chews its frozen grasses —

like gum falls apart when it's chewed too long

                a featureless lump of earth, its boneless tone
in the ground below this. Maybe it's the damage
                        that holds us together.

Fall hazard   entrapment, engulfment hazard   grain bridge collapse —

the spare sound of a logger's mallet struck
against a tree with heart rot:

a multitude of hearts rot in the echo   ring to ring.

My avatar in the poem within the poem   his hollow
shelved with bracket fungi —

tongue, beard, lip, tongue
hanging from a flowery branch scooping shade

from residential streets
or grassy banks:

a caption, a scroll

over stylized waves, azure, per fess between the folds
in its nest   a crane in its vigilance.

Fish fry specials every Friday during Lent.

The saving shame
of true things:

seasonal aisles   their smell
the feel of Formica countertops worn down to
the brown.

Continents change hands. A stub of rainbow pokes the gray sky. Still

lighthouses watch over shingle-colored rocks   the cedar siding of cottage
after cottage   their cold hearths

                 no puddles around the pump

no habit of house keys —

a faded Palm Sunday cross pinned to the sunvisor.

           No face under the visor   only geese plucking
           their names from shitty grasses —

squirrels dig old holes in the new mulch. No body in the armor.

No glaciers carving their record in the earthen table.

             Talk bubble   thought bubble —

the divers of Bikini Atoll.

         A weather-vane spins in the humid, milky

breeze of mewing sea lions. Clouds shape   reshape
       rush over tiny places

past walls, gates, arches   giant earthen mounds
              in the shape of sacred animals   cloverleafs
                                   exit ramps.

Fields of cut corn stalks and dry dirt —

              a Styrofoam airplane loops in the yard —

clouds even
      over the ocean-wrecked desert and
              brackish marsh. The storm spins.

The melt cuts riverbeds in tundra

ice floe floating the Arctics. Barren rock holds
              the icy tongues mumbling.

          Jet lines clean as a thumbnail through wax

a crease in the overcast —

          the rubbed edges of envelopes in hatboxes.

Neon lights of the corner bar. Madonna in her grotto

how rain hangs on a window, how the long aluminum fingers of wind
    chimes
                   wiggle a little.

Reserved parking   street cleaning   family plots

                                    burn barrels for raked leaves
                                       smoke up over the interstate.

Gravel, sand, and snow sprayed by the plow on the road sign

                  crusted cave formations. New sex positions.

Snow still in the longest shadows   the deepest ruts

                                    color of ash and orange pith —

a spot of oil in each parking space at NAPA Auto Parts:

knotted rainbow
       oil leaks, sweetish smell of anti-freeze. Utilities crews

                  on cherry pickers cut branches back from the lines;

sawdust spurts from branch to blade, gets caught in
                  the mesh safety vests of the flaggers.

City drivers turn their heads to look at the barn ruins.

                  Insects hook themselves on screened-in porches —

seasons pass in the butter dish.

                    The smell of ice-cream treats, fresh asphalt.

            Water spins from the wet-cutter. At the grocery store

in the box-store foyer:

coin-operated horses, cars   the pelican ride   Dumbo's ears
                                        spread like wings.

Rotisserie chickens under the heat lamps near the deli section

aisle numbers. Scorecards

                                golf pencils at the trailhead —

the sun heavy as a wooden barrel.

Spray paint blazes tree to tree. Pink matchheads.

                Wood smoke runs its fingers through the firs
                                through my hair.

Push and pull of personhood   state magnets   patina of moss
            on trees-stand camouflage.

Animals move about the sleeping bags   through tent flaps.

Children pretend to growl and hiss —

in a crackling nowhere only nobody can see:

a wall of TVs on the same channel   skiers   tropical tail-feathers

a thousand miles away.

My ears ring with the empty city.

Lawn and garden   bait and tackle   hook and hunt. Fenceposts
rotted by rainfall

or broken off in mischief.

They lean against the wire   they're held up by the wire —

bark-side lichens

soft to the touch and scalloped.

House mouse   city mouse: the beat of some other light heart.

Birds under the underpass

their distress calls taken by wind and

wing-feather. Ivy climbs over the billboard. Ivy climbs
         over the tree

               from tree to tree to tunnel clearance

highway after highway until there's no more ivy.

Adaptation of mammals back to the water   adaptation
               of cities to the brownout:

community service pulls tires from the muddy banks dumped

sidewalls brim with the last big rain. A little
               spills from the lip like tobacco spit

stagnant scum   soft like
               fur on the webbing between otters' toes.

The new hatch glitters in the fisherman's laugh.

               Friendship necklace

its jagged edge

               bearings hiss in the display case.

Truck-stop ceramics: fairy or pixie   with or without wand butterfly, dragonfly, bat, or bee

highway after highway   past souvenir shops
                                        the Indian teepee trading post.

Purple and pink sunsets on the adobes

through the federal lands — reservation
just over barbed wire twisted like a handshake   a double-helix

boneless ether above Malpaís. The ancient city

strikes an asterisk into the night   ports cut into rocky grasses —

torchlight   odor of offal   saltpeter   lime —

signet in wax or branding iron
searing the herd's rump — voter's thumbs
dipped in a special ink.

In wet weather   the rust bubbles the paint   breaks   flakes off.

How the climate fatigues the new arrivals

almost overtaken on the tarmac.

Stark shade of the desert in the hollows of the cactus skeleton.

The moon base spins through the galaxy   orbit doubled around
the blackened crater of the universe

          the hairless skin of the black hole.

Saturn's rings

          spin like hula-hoops
            more stars   twirling batons

a fist in the French horn.

Mechanics in the shade in herringbone coveralls tilt the telescopic antenna.

A wall of Fords and Packards banked against the blowing dust
            across Kansas.

Gilded pancakes at the breakfast buffet.

    A pastel dragon   resin-cast   coiled around geoid.

Garage doors open to the California skies:
          spiders descend at twilight

     from the branches of the orange grove

little green men   savages fleeing   ocean crests

crashing in folds of light   eddying
                        through the chandelier

through the internet   the vineyards of North America

international fishing waters.

                                Deckhands slip in the slush; processors

break crab legs with blood-pickled fingers.

All-you-can-eat weekends. Nail salons.

Lady Liberty holds her torch aloft in the darkness   Lady Columbia
in her robes stringing telegraph lines

                                across the territories —

rays of sun part the clouds in glory.

                I wait for her pirates to hoist a flag in my heart.

I wait for static and sleep.

Meadowland with or without wolf or wolves   wolf and child.

                First stamp of a hoof — the early warning signs.

Missiles shore to shore over the Florida Straits
preening thrust mid-flight. Fire fairy with red dragon

winter fairy with snowflake wings.

The eye in the pine-board bedframe. The frosts of
Arizona and New Mexico

unruffled sand and scrub —

the Mojave is fatherless to me.

Slow white waves erode the granite breakers: each broken crest carries

particles of island far beyond
beaches no one knows the name of
to coasts with sand soft as skin.

Bandwidth broader through radar-rich valleys

between the tunnels, over the overpass

burning candy or roasting coffee

melting plastic from an electrical fire

the stomach's acids   unwashed hair

ozone   sparks from the bumper cars   lights of the Ferris wheel
sparks on the subway tracks —

streetlights mark the routes in

and out of town at night.

Down under the Boeing wing: the empty stadium

disaster site   PCBs in the sediment pinched in space's vacuum —
a clot in the rake.

The gray, greasy flakes of a scratch-off ticket
on the edge of a penny —

Kennedy half-dollar piece.

Refineries   sewage treatment plants

transfer stations   hockey rinks. Newspapers report
life on Mars fossilized in icy oceans.

Red letters over Oklahoma   tiny as needlework.

Register receipts and circulars
in the supermarket lot blow
back and forth over the crosswalk.

Parking garage building blocks
new live / work spaces — desktop PC
replicas in the office furniture section

hollow like wax fruit —

humidity in the pedestrian walkway between the shimmering summer deals

and the couches and recliners. Past the gown section

men's dress suits   the shoe section

kiddie clothes

down the escalators beyond the matte white mannequins
in seasonal fashions:

the tremble of a new scent   rustle of heavy gauge paper bags

nylon rope handles through
their grommets.

Carousel music   mirrors   rows of incandescent fixtures:

horse   dolphin   seal
swan   leopard   tiger   horse   dragon   horse   zebra   camel

tiger   horse   giraffe   a cat with a fish in its mouth —

a grin jumps in the mirrors.

The brass poles twist into the canopy.

Fluorescents buzz in the dressing room —

the department store tucked into the Fairy Queen's purse as

flesh-tones clear a way through glittering air.

Gods once took the shape of animals
and animals once gods themselves

gliding from body to body under
colossi after colossi.

Buffalo, wolf   bear, thunderbird. When the people are asleep
coyotes hunt the byways

learn the habits of the suburbs

travel to and from the city by human routes, past shop windows

more mannequins between outfits:

blank pubis pushed out toward the storefront glass.

Casey's   Quik Trip   76 — sunrise on masonry
                        the color of a dog's tongue.

Through a hole in the air
                     a giant squid throws its limbs
around the splintering ship. Pegasus takes flight

       a halo of stars spins around the mountain peak

lion roars   flag flies —

    static   black seaweed   only bigger

              like a thigh in the dark

underwater fruits ripening until gathered   there where
one part of the Earth covers the other

      as with the borrowed shell of the hermit crab

its whiskery legs fold up into a fist, spread out over wet sand —

        boardwalk backdrop

jogger's faces slack with strain   Frisbees   weightlifters   beauty queens

Hanes classics   Maidenform   Everlast. Eve series:

Cameo White finish with abstract head
fingers   right hand on hip   turned at waist

slightly bent left leg. The crosswalk chirps
ripples patient in the middle of the street.

Lemonade   white wine   Wikipedia   sphagnum moss   trained doves
clouds seeded with moments lost like

twin caves   islands to each other   cut off except by waterfalls.

The universe expands faster
tugs constellations from their tethers —

the return of Aquaman   Pam Anderson   Tudor architecture.

Cigarette butts at the loading docks — manifestation of anxiety
in the muscles of the face, sinus, anus.

Doves return to their roost
so much post returned to sender.

CBs squawk. From behind the police barriers
along the funeral route

citizens wave flags
citizens choke with emotion

along the parade route after the storm:
                    the palms' petticoats are heavy with rain and

                    street debris:

utensils   flattened water bottles   paper plates   noise-makers
confetti poppers   halves of fresh squeezed oranges

                                        ice dumped from a cooler

star-shaped glasses   grains of sugar and cinnamon from churros.

                    The track of an ant in dry dirt

its footprints smaller than a pinhole
                    in a map of the archipelago.

Then the dream dives like a fish on the line or a paper airplane
        keel of vessel.

            An octopus fondles the ocean floor; a whale

swells the surface with its tail. Little necks plant their stalks —

        Tortuga's pigeons peck their bittering seed. A gull
                    skims the wave with its wing.

Alpine butterfly   running bowline   halyard hitch   greenhorn keeping straight which is which —

                                        decline of epaulettes. Barnacles

grow on the crusted iron lung. Their feathery legs waving

                        around their buried mouth.

My ears pop with the change in cabin pressure. Tectonic plates

slide together one beneath the other —
                                        bacteria humps up into little hills:

strobe lights at the beginning of life.

Pearly foam   floating ice — the Arctic origin of seals
                                                whales   mackerel.

Flying fish flop on deck. Stars reflected like drops

of water hang from the cave ceiling — the cave's bilge

tannins from the forest floor color the deposits.

                                Streaks of magnesium   iron

                        leech like fingers through a rug's fringes
                        smell of candles and Sterno. The kite dips

                                        its string slackens some.

A slideshow of the exhibition:
                    the first photos of Inuits
                                furs pulled back.

I'm wringing a string around the tea bag in the teaspoon.

The Alaskan scoops caviar from a salmon belly — berries
                                            through the fog.

Tree roots grow
                        farther from the trunk
                        nearer the foundation

crush the basement like a corsage — wisteria runners

crack the pipes. After prom
                    the purple shape of a hand around an arm

or a handful of dirt tossed on the coffin of a loved one.

            The birthday boy gets the corner piece of the cake —

fear of stray dogs, empty paper-wasp nests. Houseplants in
                        their natural environments

in another hemisphere

the unbruised body of the Chairman laid in state
his waxen organs sealed with a sickle of golden stars.

Wind in the straw   slave hands
        heavy with mud, mortar, seed —
                human limbs gnashed in root   rock

under sluggish raindrops   under thunder   layover —

scuffs from shoes, broken luggage wheels

        customer care carts' sudden stop   start
          change of tone from tile to carpet —

QR codes   boarding passes

    the beat of an unmoored heart in the duty-free shop.

Vacuums leave their pattern; windows steamed up
                around the boarding gates.

        The mountains far off

through dust kicked up in a color I've grown to love —

the moon of this moon
behind the rocks   the war-whoop of these alien birds:

former selves perched before
the source of being

or a shadowy imprint born again unrecognizable to friends

haunted by films of
other lives in gingham or windowpane plaid
lives uncoiling like

sleepy, cold lizards emerge to sun on the rocks.

I draw a dotted line to the moon, follow it with a scissors.

Oscar award   distress beacon

astral projection

borrowed names burrowing like baby beetles from dung

their bubble
rolled along the course of the Milky Way

along the Rio Grande. Then the American eagle displayed proper
two rifles with bayonets in its talons.

Passenger manifest   customs declaration
the colors of Sunday cartoons

Jeffy hops through trees

                    in and out of buckets, birdbaths

over fences   over teeter-totters

      in and out of dog houses. Jeffy bounces through the tulips —

           · so the sailor through the grassy waves

     water deep in the beaches' breach

fish by fish

     the shoal spins and splits

                unlike how birds circle their prey

        that spiral staircase

winding into the very middle of my being not exactly me anymore but

           sullen seas stitched together
           like satin stretched over pillows.

Alcatraz   the last match of the blackout. Then this very word
poking into pure white-hot creation.

         Routine weather   cashiers   mail-trucks

cargo planes   a map of the globe   flashlights   hairbrushes
handwash only delicates —

       little tabs and flags
          stuck in the cross section at Muir woods

                  like a conquest.

Tourists transported through the redwood agape —

       a human being driven straight through the life of the tree

a redwood grown straight through the life of a human being

more human beings scattered like
          new nails dumped from a box.

A year's rain in soil: a new ring inscribed
          by the fall of water from the sky.

Arrowhead   confluence — plywood over busted windows.

        The way water puddles differently in different cities
        how trees hold rain, how

    buildings carry rain
around flashing and chimneys. How fog settles or wanders —

how dew gems grass or pregnancy tests.

And then the confluence
presses down on the heart of the continent.

Pine-needled mud under a wet tissue:

condensation in a plastic bag full of trash
        stuffed in the rotted top of a cut-off phone pole.

Guard rail tagged, tagged again.

Lighthouse families
bead the coastline with swinging mirrors that never land on land.

An eroding bank gripped in roots' mossy fists —
the circumference of a hull   a pit

radar radius floating   tossed   starlit

shore-wrecked
                into the compass, the calipers

centuries of frozen ice down the crystal lattice of the universe —

a picture in a locket's frame
                that loveless location. Mourning doves in twos
                        at the widow's perch   as if

trees had no roots, the ocean no currents   as if grain could grow
in prow cut furrows.

      Barbs of goose down prick through the thread count.

                The evening tide pulls swash
over the heads of those who died
          undressing weather-women with their eyes.

The minister's secretary unfolds the paperclip from

      the bottom of the drawer — the targeting program

searches the millionth chamber of
          the reef's bleached bark for a sweet spot

in the seabed shale. Somewhere past the space debris
              and bridal magazines:

the smell of chamomile growing in the gravel
          of mice in the grain in
     the silo's froth.

Bubbles in the latex paint expand against the sheetrock.

             Offshore princes in corner offices
        prance witty   clean as scrubbed clams —

clenched as bunting in cold rain. Finger roulette underdeck
                                          in the tanker's blink.

The different tones of different lights. DVDs in the media cabinet
          in the mess room.

                              My hands smell of mustard
                                   from the sandwich.

The whale's eye black in inky enmity — the burrowing barnacle

or the Carlotta drawn to the wrong lights:

                              hull grinning ear to ear to be
                              nearer things heard from outer space.

Her hair still wet in the center of the ponytail —

the robin's breast color of the nebula's little belly   the coral pattern

                    in a Kansas rock-outcrop

menthol butts in the parking lot. Fried peanuts. Aluminum.

Eminent domain. Headstones pulled out by the root. Between

          basin and range, derricks in the vineyard

pound the chest of the first victim of time travel —

pockets full of permafrost jiggling like jelly

mammoths thawing soft as plant rot.

Heavy metals at the crash site:

boutonnière in the corner of the fire circle —

sunshine through fungus-covered branches

a burr stuck to a striped sock with some kind of pattern on it.

Stacks of roofing shingles. The smell of bruised petals

different colored
spatter of clover and dandelion

patches of devil's paintbrush sprayed by the mower.

Weather balloons   atmosphere — water towers, linear move or
central pivot irrigation systems

washes   sluices.

Depots near the docks near the tracks   lumberyard near the mill
near the old path of the river like a crooked finger.

The construction crew sprays down the demolition site to keep
        the dust from drifting.

The chemical plant outside city limits burns bald the fenced-up banks

the lightning zigs and zags   a drop from a vial of liquid bites into a hand.

            Different tones to different bridges.

Dredges sort particle by particle

                through the bladder's bloody body of water

                    the human liver   the size of a

shoebox for a frog — rain in the leafy gutter
wet wood under the shelter. Ants dry in the core of the log.

                Petals curl back under their own weight

curl more under the weight of water.

Juniper trees grow twisted in the Pacific breeze that
                        separates bark from flesh.

            Soap and shampoo from the outdoor showers
    in the backyards of the cedar-clapped Cape Cods froth
                in the runoff.

Napkins flutter under silverware.

Edgar, matte finish, hands by side   right leg slightly forward.

Tall child   headless   white.

Square bale props. Blue skies marble backdrop. Spit bubbles

signs of home on my tongue

through fathoms no secrets rise up to meet me.

In the tidal pool

where sparklers tickle the unlit faces

pinch their fingers,

the moon cuts time

into portions   souvenirs — snow globes.

An orange peel studded with cloves
in a pot of water on the wood-stove.

The seamless walls of grain elevators
power plant chimneys   the legs of the rig —

concrete mix poured ceaseless into

the ceaselessly moving frame. My heart turns like
blown glass in tongs.

The door pushes open and
rings the shopkeeper's bell.

The ear cocked   almost lost in the lasting
signs of Danish beauty in the hand-painted porcelain provenance:

clamdiggers   milkmaids
Jersey cow lying down.

Girl with lost balloon in Mary blue. Figurine of a

Greenlandic girl with bouquet — hand-painted
stem by stem.

Girl feeding calf from bucket   shepherd boy cutting a stick.

Sealand girl with garland in regional costume

overglazed, a few chips on the flowers. Bing & Grøndahl
girl figurine

standing with spilt milk, underglaze. Girl sitting with

doll on her arm.

Woman with fishing net looking to the far. Girl with

mirror   faun and nymph   kneeling, kissing —
                    Gerhard Henning   1909.

Fanoe   Jutland   Bornholm   Amager —
                    the Shepherdess and the Sweep.

                    The music box plays as it unwinds.

Bathing girl, how the water is so cold — faun (satyr or Pan)

with frog   with snake   with owl   with crow   with rabbit
                                    lizard   squirrel.

The sandman stands with his umbrella above Helena

                    nude girl with mirror, underglaze.

Boy riding on goat — mermaid on rock, shepherd boy on rock
                    looking to the herd, old women collecting potatoes.

Faun playing flute. Milkmaid girl

                    walking with a sheaf of straw, girl with book —

white skin like fog in my eyes. Factory marks   painter's numbers.

Two girls with book — twins going to sleep.

Three blue waves
        stamped in red or green on base. "The Flight to America"

girl and boys going to the Land of the Free,

                Christian Thomsen, underglazed, 21 cm.

A trail of gasoline carried by rainwater
                floats like a signature
                        down the curb to the storm drain.

Click of heels   shuffle of shoes. An umbrella flaps,
        inside a beckoning cat beckons with a bobbing paw.

                I ring the bell on the counter. Tea roses

stem roses   carnations   lilies   Delphinium   Feverfew   sweet peas
sword fern   babies breath

                A boy with flowers for
                his first love. Claire Weiss, underglazed, 19 cm —

marked with three Royal Towers of Copenhagen. Rustle of wrapping
                                paper

the zip of a gift ribbon being curled with a scissor blade. Over the faux
      fence

            through the glass in the florist's fridge

I watch a face among the buckets
               hover between arrangements. Such a spy

need only open the door
            to enter our world and a little cooler

     sweeter-smelling air follows him in.

ACKNOWLEDGMENTS

This project emerged from road travel between St. Louis and Los Angeles, San Francisco, Detroit, Minneapolis, Cleveland, Kansas City, Pittsburgh, and Fort Wayne as well as time spent in Cape Cod, the Hudson Valley, Mark Twain National Forrest, the Mojave National Preserve and other places around the country that have impressed imagery into the poem. Thank you to all who have read the poem in manuscript and encouraged its voice, including Filip Marinovich, Ted Mathys, Matvei Yankelevich, Devin Johnston, and especially Kyra Simone and Daniel Owen whose enthusiasm for the project has shaped my confidence. Thanks you also to to Nathan Cook for including a lengthy excerpt of *Lost Horizon* in *Bruxism* #10. Abiding gratitude goes to Julien Poirier for his insights into one of the earliest iterations of the poem and especially to Jessica Baran for her guidance and support through countless restless revisions.

COLOPHON

This is the first edition and first printing of *Lost Horizon*, copyright 2019 by Nathaniel Farrell, published by Ugly Duckling Presse, Brooklyn, New York, and distributed by Small Press Distribution, Berkeley, California. The book was printed offset on archival, partially-recycled papers and bound in an edition of one thousand copies at McNaughton & Gunn in Saline, Michigan, using cover stock from French Paper Company, Niles, Michigan. *Lost Horizon* was designed and typeset by Don't Look Now!, Doormouse, and Kyra Simone. The type is Dante and Frutiger.

Ugly Duckling Presse is a 501(c)(3) nonprofit publisher of poetry, translation, invbestigative works, and performance texts. The publication of this book was made possible in part by a grant from the National Endowment for the Arts and support from the New York State Council on the Arts, a state agency.

Ugly Duckling Presse
The Old American Can Factory
232 Third Street, #E-303
Brooklyn, New York 11215

www.uglyducklingpresse.org